First Facts

Who Lived Here?

RIVER
Communities
PAST and PRESENT

by Danielle Smith-Llera

Consultant:
Zoe Burkholder, PhD
Assistant Professor, College of Education
and Human Services
Montclair State University
Montclair, New Jersey

CAPSTONE PRESS
a capstone imprint

First Facts are published by Capstone Press,
1710 Roe Crest Drive, North Mankato, Minnesota 56003
www.capstonepub.com

Library of Congress Cataloging-in-Publication Data
Smith-Llera, Danielle, 1971–
River communities past and present / by Danielle Smith-Llera.
     pages cm. — (First facts. Who lived here?)
Summary: "Compares and contrasts the way people lived near a
North American river over the course of centuries"—Provided by
publisher.
Includes bibliographical references and index.
  ISBN 978-1-4765-4058-0 (library binding)
  ISBN 978-1-4765-5140-1 (paperback)
  ISBN 978-1-4765-5993-3 (eBook PDF)
1. Rivers—Juvenile literature. 2. Human geography—Juvenile
literature. 3. Stream ecology—Juvenile literature. I. Title.
GF63.S65 2014
307.0973—dc23   2013035319

Editorial Credits
Brenda Haugen, editor; Juliette Peters, designer; Svetlana Zhurkin,
media researcher; Charmaine Whitman, production specialist

Photo Credits
Alamy: Niday Picture Library, 21, North Wind Picture Archives, 7, 9,
11, 13, 15; iStockphotos: xavierarnau, 20; Library of Congress, cover
(log cabin), 17; National Geographic Creative: Roy Andersen, 5;
Shutterstock: Anne Kitzman, 19, Samiah Samin (background), cover
and throughout, Samuel Borges Photography, cover (middle back), 1,
2, 23, 24, Stanislav Komogorov, cover (left)

Printed in the United States of America in North Mankato, Minnesota.
092013   007771CGS14

TABLE OF CONTENTS

AN IMPORTANT FOOD SOURCE 4

RELYING ON THE RIVER 6

TRADING ON THE RIVER 8

EUROPEAN SETTLERS ARRIVE 10

THE RIVER POWERS FACTORIES 12

CONNECTING WATERWAYS 14

RELYING LESS ON THE RIVER 16

POLLUTION BECOMES A PROBLEM . . . 18

APPRECIATING THE RIVER 20

AMAZING BUT TRUE! 21

Glossary 22

Read More 23

Internet Sites 23

Critical Thinking Using
    the Common Core 24

Index 24

AN IMPORTANT FOOD SOURCE

8000 BC

Rivers have always been an important resource for people. But how they used the resource has changed over time.

In ancient times people settled near rivers because they provided a food source. They collected oysters and caught crabs by hand. Fish swam into nets weighted down with stones.

During the winter months, parts of the rivers froze. People carved tools from large stones found near rivers. They used the tools to cut holes in the ice to fish.

People live by a river in ancient times.

FACT

People shaped river clay into pots to store their food.

RELYING ON THE RIVER
1300s

In the 1300s American Indians built canoes to use on the river. Canoes carried the men to battle against their enemies. People from different villages gathered together to fish and feast along the river.

RIVER STORIES

American Indians often told **myths** about rivers and the beginning of life. They believed the great **spirit** wandered the dry Earth and suffered from great thirst. According to the story, the great spirit cried tears that became streams and rivers.

myth—a story told by people in ancient times; myths often tried to explain natural events

spirit—an invisible being

Men fished with spears and hooks. Women cooked the fish in underground pits. They scattered leftover fish on nearby fields to make the soil **rich**. River flooding made the soil rich too. People grew **crops** in the soil.

rich—having many nutrients to help plants grow

crop—a plant farmers grow in large amounts, usually for food

TRADING ON THE RIVER
1600s

In the 1600s European explorers sailed on rivers and traded with American Indians. The explorers brought glass beads, tools, tobacco, guns, and bullets. In exchange, the American Indians traded the soft furs they wore.

The explorers filled boats with furs. They brought the furs down the rivers to the Atlantic Ocean. Ships carried the furs to Europe. Fur hats were popular in shops there. Most American Indians spent their days trapping animals instead of farming to fill the demand for fur.

Europeans explorers meet with American Indians along the Hudson River in 1609.

EUROPEAN SETTLERS ARRIVE

1700s

Hundreds of Europeans traveled on rivers to start new lives in North America in the 1700s. They built businesses called mills by rivers. The water turned wheels in the mills to make power. The power was used to grind grain and cut wood. Flour and lumber were sent downriver to ocean **ports**. Sugar and tools from other countries were sent upriver to the new settlements.

---

port—a place where boats and ships can dock safely

THE RIVER POWERS FACTORIES

LATE 1700s AND EARLY 1800s

People built **dams** on rivers to help power factory machines in the late 1700s and early 1800s. More goods than ever flowed downstream on cargo ships.

FAST RIVERS GROW CITIES

Fast-moving waterfalls produced a lot of power for factories along rivers in the 1800s. As the factories grew, jobs were created. Towns near fast-flowing waters grew larger and wealthier more quickly than those along slowly moving rivers. These bigger towns grew into important cities, such as Albany and New York.

Cargo is loaded onto riverboats in Cincinnati, Ohio.

European **immigrants** sailed upstream on returning cargo ships. River towns buzzed with many languages. People found jobs in factories making iron stoves, glass, and leather goods.

dam—a wall that stretches across a river; it slows down the rushing water and raises the water level behind it

immigrant—a person who leaves one country and settles in another

CONNECTING WATERWAYS

1800s

Canals were dug to connect rivers and lakes in the 1800s. These new connections allowed **barges** to carry factory goods to more places. Mules walked beside canals and pulled barges that carried up to 240 tons (218 metric tons) of products.

People moved to canal towns to find jobs. They worked on the docks and built new boats.

canal—a channel that is dug across land; canals connect bodies of water so that ships can travel between them

barge—a large, flat ship used to transport goods

A mule team pulls a grain boat on the Erie Canal.

FACT

It took eight years to build the Erie Canal in New York. The men working on the canal earned 80 cents to $1 per day.

RELYING
LESS ON THE RIVER
LATE 1800s

Steam power made rivers less important in the late 1800s. Steam-powered trains rumbled down tracks laid alongside canals and rivers. People could travel and send goods more cheaply and quickly by train.

HARD LIVES IN FACTORIES

New families arriving in river towns needed to earn enough money for housing, food, and clothing. Often every member had to work in a factory so the family could survive. Even children worked 12 hours a day.

A steamboat makes its way up a river as a steam-powered train carries goods on land in St. Louis, Missouri.

Factories were powered by steam made from pools of still water. Workers could now live and work in towns far from riverbanks.

POLLUTION BECOMES A PROBLEM

Towns and factories dumped their waste into rivers. When factories burned coal, **acid rain** fell into the rivers. When power plants made electricity from river currents, dangerous chemicals escaped.

Pollution settled deep into the riverbeds. Drinking river water and eating fish made people sick. Laws were passed to make dumping factory waste into rivers **illegal**.

---

acid rain—rain, snow, or fog that contains acids made from pollutants mixing with water in the air

pollution—materials that hurt Earth's water, air, and land

illegal—against the law

APPRECIATING THE RIVER

Today rivers are used for business and for fun. Water flows through spinning **turbines** on dams, making electricity without pollution. Barges still carry goods on rivers. People fish, paddle on rivers in canoes, and have picnics on the riverbanks.

People try to keep rivers clean. Dangerous chemicals are soaked up from rivers with huge sponges. Everyone treasures healthy rivers.

turbine—an engine powered by steam or gas

Fast-moving water and waterfalls did not stop boats from using rivers. This was especially true in the Hudson River Valley in New York. In the late 1700s and early 1800s several canals were built on the river. The canals helped boats travel from hilly areas to flat ones.

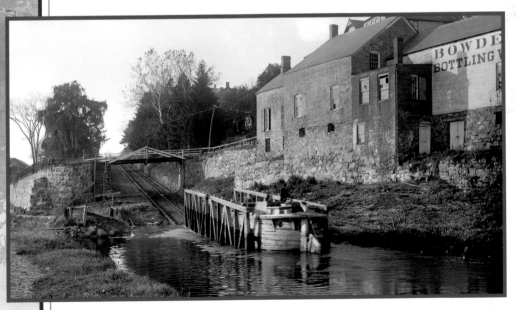

GLOSSARY

acid rain (A-suhd RAYN)—rain, snow, or fog that contains acids made from pollutants mixing with water in the air

barge (BARJ)—a large, flat ship used to transport goods

canal (kuh-NAL)—a channel that is dug across land; canals connect bodies of water so that ships can travel between them

crop (KROP)—a plant farmers grow in large amounts, usually for food

dam (DAM)—a wall that stretches across a river; it slows down the rushing water and raises the water level behind it

illegal (i-LEE-guhl)—against the law

immigrant (IM-uh-gruhnt)—a person who leaves one country and settles in another

myth (MITH)—a story told by people in ancient times; myths often tried to explain natural events

pollution (puh-LOO-shuhn)—materials that hurt Earth's water, air, and land

port (PORT)—a place where boats and ships can dock safely

rich (RICH)—having many nutrients to help plants grow

spirit (SPIHR-it)—an invisible being

turbine (TUR-bine)—an engine powered by steam or gas

READ MORE

Nunn, Daniel. *Water.* Why Living Things Need. Chicago: Heinemann-Raintree, 2012.

Talbott, Hudson. *River of Dreams: The Story of the Hudson River.* New York: G.P. Putnam's Sons, 2009.

Waldron, Melanie. *Rivers.* Habitat Survival. Chicago: Heinemann-Raintree, 2012.

INTERNET SITES

FactHound offers a safe, fun way to find Internet sites related to this book. All of the sites on FactHound have been researched by our staff.

Here's all you do:

Visit *www.facthound.com*

Type in this code: 9781476540580

Super-cool stuff!

Check out projects, games and lots more at
www.capstonekids.com

CRITICAL THINKING USING THE COMMON CORE

1. How did canals help cities and towns grow? (Key Ideas and Details)

2. Look at the sidebar "River Stories" on page 6. What is the author trying to explain in this sidebar? (Craft and Structure)

INDEX

Atlantic Ocean, 8

barges, 14, 20

canals, 14, 15, 16, 21
canoes, 6, 20

dams, 12, 20

Europe, 8
explorers, 8

factories, 12, 13, 14, 16, 17, 18
farming, 7, 8
fishing, 4, 6, 7, 20
food, 4, 6, 7, 18

immigrants, 13

mills, 10
myths, 6

North America, 10

pollution, 18, 20
ports, 10

ships, 8, 12, 13

tools, 4, 7, 8
trade, 8
trains, 16
trapping, 8
turbines, 20

waterfalls, 12, 21